GREAT GLASGOW JOKES

AND ONE LINERS

LangSyne
PUBLISHING
WHERE FUN BEGINS!

1.

Mrs McGinty went out to the shops leaving the parrot in charge of the household. The gas meter reader chapped the door and the parrot screeched, "Who izzit?" "I've come to read the gas meter," came the response. Again the parrot screeched, "Who izzit?" This exchange was repeated numerous times until the gas man got fed up and was about to move on when he heard the front door of the tenement open. He called out his identity and Mrs McGinty, a bit hard of hearing, shouted: "Who izzit?" And from the living room the parrot screeched: "It's the gas man. He's come to read the meter."

The harassed mammy was registering for universal credit and the clerk had some questions "How many children do you have?" "10". "Their names?" "Harry, Harry, Harry, Harry, Harry, Harry, Harry, Harry, Harry…and Harry." "All the same name, doesn't that get confusing, what happens if you want just to call one of them if they are out in the street playing?" "Aw that's easy," says the maw, "Ah just shout their surname."

3.

Give me a quid or you're getting stabbed, threatened the geezer on Argyle Street.
"I thought – quite reasonable."
Kevin Bridges.

Jimmy takes a pair of shoes back to the shop because a lace is missing. The bored counter assistant says, "Naw, look at the label, it says Taiwan.

Archie's Primary 5 teacher was taken aback to spot a used condom lying on a verandah just outside the classroom window. She called Jake the janitor hoping he could remove it discreetly.

But Jake was a bit hard of hearing and spoke in a loud voice. “Whit? A used condom did ye say? Oan the verandah?” Needless to say the entire class heard. Job done and janitor away teacher was conscious of a couple of dozen pairs of quizzical eyes upon her. Sure enough, Archie put his hand up. “Please miss whit’s a verandah?”

Fuctifano – polite response when the Glaswegian can’t answer a question.

Mary was in Burntisland for the Glesca Fair Fortnight and had her fortune told at the shows. “You will suffer great hardship for 10 years,” said the gypsy wife. “And then what?” asked Mary. “Then you’ll get used to it.”

What happened to the guy who liked to eat bricks and cement? He’s awa noo.

Stranger in the Southside:"Excuse me please – where's the nearest boozer?" Southsider: "You're talking to him mate."

What do you call an illegitimate Glasgow insect? A wee fly bastard.

Dave decided to enter the carpet trade – because he had a flair for it.

12.

Dougie walks into a clothing shop in Patrick and asks for a pair of gloves. The assistant asks,what fur. "Tae keep ma hauns warm," he replies.

13.

At a pub quiz in Drumchapel the last question to

win the £1,000 prize was: "Take That's first Album had a four word title, the first two words were, "Take That, what were the second two?" After a long silence Big Hughie stands up and asks, "Was it…Ya Bastard?"

14.

Glasgow audiences were hard to please in the theatres of old, many patrons taking rotten fruit to throw at comedians who failed to make them laugh. A London drag artiste was having a particularly hard time until a gallant Weegie came to the rescue and pleaded with the audience, "Aw come oan, gie the poor old coo a chance!"

15.

Great all round entertainer, the late Johnny Beattie appeared as the dame in more than 30 pantomime productions. "I have been Nurse Bella Donna, Nurse Penny Sillin, Nurse Ophelia Pulse and Nurse Phillipa Bedpan!" he said.

16.

Auld faither used to tell us:"As weans we were so poor we couldn't afford shoes. Ma da used to paint oor feet black and lace up oor toes."

17.

Glasgow, the city where you can destroy someone's credibility with just one word.... SHITE!!!

18.

Mammy to her teenage daughter: "Some day you will meet a man who will sweep you off your feet and promise you the world. Punch the lying bastard as hard as you can and run!"

19.

The well dressed man arrives at the West End brothel and asks if he can see Veronica. "Veronica is very expensive," says the madam.

"Her charge is £5,000 a visit. Are you sure?" "Yes," says the man, "I know that. The £5,000 I have is for Veronica." And he hands over the cash and has an enjoyable time. He returns the next night and asks for Veronica. Again he has a good time. Then he goes back for the third night in a row and enjoys the pleasure of Veronica's company. As he is getting dressed she asks, "This is the first time I have had three visits like this, given my prices one visit is usually it. Where are you from?" "Edinburgh," replies the man. "I have family there," says Veronica. "I know," replies the man. "Your uncle died and left you £15,000. As his solicitor and executor of the estate he instructed me to deliver the cash to you in person." All of which is confirmation of two certainties in life. Death and being screwed by a lawyer!

The F word in Glasgow: Glaswegians don't exclaim: "Really?" They exclaim: "Fuck Off!"

21.

Who discovered you get milk from cows and what did he think he was doing at the time?
Billy Connolly.

22.

Tommy Morgan (1898-1958) was a hugely successful Glasgow comedian in the first half of the 20th century. He told the story of the couple who had to vacate their East End tenement when air raid sirens sounded during the war. Half way down the street the wife shouted: "Ah hive tae go back tae the hoose – ah forgoat ma teeth," to which her exasperated husband retorted: "For goad's sake wummin, its bombs they're drappin, no sandwiches!".

23.

A lad tells his pal he is getting married and plans to wear the kilt. "What's the tartan?" his pal asks. "Oh, she'll be wearing white," he replies.

24.

A wee wummin goes to the dentist and settles down in the chair. "Comfy?" the dentist asks. "Govan," she replies.

25.

A group of friends had booked a mini bus to pick them up from outside a city centre pub (after they had imbibed a few swallies) to take them out to Daldowie Crematorium for a pal's funeral. Or so they thought. Owing to a mix-up, none of them had actually made a booking. Frantic efforts were made to arrange transport and, just in the nick of time, they managed to hire a small coach. Unfortunately, emblazoned along its side was the cheeky slogan *Your Wee Happy Bus*.

26.

Las Vegas and Glasgow have a lot in common. They are the only two places in the world where you can pay for sex with chips. *Frankie Boyle*.

27.

Hughie and Shuggie live in identical tenement flats. Hughie tells Shuggie that he has just wall-papered his kitchen. Shuggie says he has been thinking of doing the same and asks him how much paper he got. “Eight rolls”, says Hughie. Sometime later, the pals meet up in the pub. An aggrieved Shuggie challenges his friend saying, “Here you! I had two and a half rolls of paper left ower.” “Aye,” says Hughie, “so did I.”

28.

Two cars collide and the vehicles are badly dented. Fortunately no one is injured. As the drivers exchange details it emerges one is a Rangers fan and one is a Celtic fan. The Rangers fan notices a bottle of whisky in a gift bag on the back seat has survived in tact. “Why don’t we have a wee swally to celebrate no one being injured and the bottle still being in one piece?” says the Rangers fan. “Aye, nae bother,” says the Celtic fan who then proceeds to take a good dram. He then hands the bottle to the Rangers fan. "No fur me," says the Rangers fan, "Ah'll just wait for the polis."

29.

If you're lucky enough to be a Glaswegian then you're lucky enough!

30.

I had a tragic childhood. My parents never understood me. They were Japanese.
Chic Murray.

31.

A Celtic fan and a Rangers fan find a magic lamp and when the Celtic fan rubs it the genie appears. "Who rubbed the lamp?" asked the genie. "Me!" said the excited Celtic fan. "Then I will grant you three wishes but what ever you receive your friend here will get double. "I wish for a million pounds," says the Celt. "Granted and to your opposing fan two million. Second wish?"

"A Maserati." "Granted and to your opposing fan two Maseratis. And your final wish?" "Okay, I would like to donate a kidney," says the Celt.

32.

So there I was lying in the gutter. A man stopped and asked, "What's the matter. Did you fall over?" So I said, "No. I've a bar of toffee in my back pocket and I was just trying to break it." *Chic Murray*.

33.

Edinburgh and Glasgow, two very different cities. When a gun goes off in Edinburgh it's one o' clock. *Kevin Bridges*.

34.

The invention of square-toed shoes was to enable the Glasgow man to get closer to the bar. *Jack House*.

35.

A woman walks into a baker's shop and, studying the display asks, "Is that a doughnut or a meringue?" "Naw, ye were right the first time hen," the baker tells her.

36.

What did Dracula get when he came to Glasgow? A bat in the mooth.

37.

Glasgow is a very negative place. If Kayne was born in Glasgow he would have been called No You Cannae. *Frankie Boyle*.

38.

"My father was a simple man. My mother was a simple woman. You see the result standing in front of you – a simpleton. *Chic Murray*.

39.

Never trust a man who left alone with a tea cosy, doesn't try it on. *Billy Connolly.*

40.

The prisoner was lonely in Barlinnie. He was in his cell.

41.

There are nine coos in a field, which one's the nearest to Iraq? Coo eight.

42.

A young teacher who was a recent incomer to Glasgow asked her class where they lived. "Ah live in a boat hoose," one wee lad proudly replied. "That's very interesting," the teacher said, "Where's it moored. On the Clyde?" "Naw," the bemused lad replies, "It's a boat hoose...ma dad boat it aff the cooncil.

43.

In Glasgow, 'how' means 'why'. You do not ponder why. You demand HOW? *Kevin Bridges.*

44.

Inebriated and broke, a man is walking down the street when he sees a motorist trying to fix his broken down car. "What's up pal?" he asks. "Piston broke" he is informed. "Aye, same as masel," the man dolefully replies.

45.

It's a small world but I wouldn't want to paint it... *Chic Murray.*

46.

Three of us went to a fancy dress party in Glasgow last night, dressed as a giant sandwich. We managed to get home in one piece... *Sanjeev Kohli.*

47.

There are four cows in a field – which is the one that's on holiday? The one with the wee calf.

48.

Mary Doll just asked me: "Whit ye daen for Easter?" And I told her, "The same thing Jesus done. I'm gonny disappear on Friday and reappear on Monday…" *Rab C Nesbitt*.

49.

Tae a' Fart – Hawd yir Bum Tight Tae the Chair Tae Try and Stop the Leakin' Air – Shift yir Ass Fae Cheek tae Cheek And Pray Tae God It Doesny Reek! *Billy Connolly*.

50.

A young woman phones her dad after a night out and asks if he can come and pick her up. She's missed her last bus home and the rain is teeming down. "Okay" her dad replies, "where are you ringing from?" "Frae the tap of ma heid right doon tae ma knickers!"

51.

The police stopped me when I was in my car. They said it was a spot check. I admitted to two pimples and a boil. *Chic Murray*.

52.

Where can you see possums in Glasgow? Possumpark.

53.

A letter arrived at a city sorting office addressed to God. It asked for £50 to buy Christmas presents for two poor weans living on the breadline. Moved, the staff had a whip round and raised £45 which was posted to the address on the letter. A week later a thank you note arrived which concluded: "Ah need tae tell ye it was £5 short, ah blame they thievin' bastards at the post office."

54.

A fart is your arse applauding.
Billy Connolly.

55.

Big Wullie frae Brigton wis huvvin a rerr time on his Fair Fortnight in Rothesay. At the B & B he shouted down to the landlady: "There's nae towel here with which to dry ma hauns!" "Ye dinna need a towel – ye can hing yer hauns oot the windae," she replied. "Ach, its jist as weel ah'm no haein a bath!" shouted Big Wullie.

56.

Isa McDade was anxious to see her husband again when she arrived in Heaven after departing this earth. He had gone some 20 years earlier with a deathbed plea asking her to remain faithful to his memory. The angel asked for some clues as to husband Jimmy's identity. "Oh my, ma memory is a bit faded noo, but he used to say 'Ah'll turn in ma grave if you're unfaithful to me efter ah'm awa'". "I've got yow now," replied the angel. "You're looking for Birling McDade."

57.

Bonnie Prince Charlie was the only man named after three sheep dogs. *Billy Connoly.*

58.

The sprightly old spinster from Auchenshuggle, on her way home from Lourdes, had nothing to declare at Customs. A spot check was carried out after she confirmed the only bottle in her baggage contained holy water. But a few moments later the bemused Customs man produced a bottle of whisky from inside her cardigan. "Praise be!" declared the old lady. "Another miracle."

59.

Teacher to her class in Dennistoun: "It takes seven sheep to make a sweater. Wee Andy: "Please miss, ah wisnae aware they could knit."

Police were called to a domestic in Shawlands. "I gather you and your wife have been having some words, from what the neighbours tell us," said the officer. "No exactly,"said the husband, "Ah had some words but ah didnae get a chance tae yase them."

An Englishman stopped Hamish in Sauchiehall Street and begged a tenner for his fare south. "Here's £50," said Hamish. "Take another four with you!"

New Barlinnie prisoner Billy was given a bucket of water with the instructions from the warder: "That's to clean your cell." Later the warder returned and was amazed to see Billy having a bath. "Whit's goan oan here." he asked. "Geezabreak," said Billy. "Ah'm jist obeyin' yer order tae clean masel."

It was a pretty posh place. They were so used to fur coats that two bears strolled in and ordered lunch and nobody even noticed. *Chic Murray*.

Ask nae questions ye'll be telt nae lies,
Shut yer mooth and ye'll catch nae flies.

I don't know why I should have to learn algebra – I'm never likely to go there. *Billy Connolly*.

Don't mess with Glasgow people. They are temperamental. Half temper and half mental.

A cement mixer collided with a prison van on the Clydeside Expressway. Drivers are asked to be on the lookout for 16 hardened criminals.

A priest finds a dead pig on the road and alerts the police. "Did you read him his last rites?" asked the somewhat arrogant sergeant who took the call. "Naw", said the priest, "I thought I would inform the next of kin first."

It is a tough call having to throw the ball back to a group of wee Glesca lads playing fitba on the green. Get it right and you're a hero; get it wrong and you're a laughing stock!

Two teenagers were rushed to the Royal

Infirmary after taking an illegal drug that had been laced with curry powder. One was in a serious condition, the other in a korma

71.

What do you call a Glasgow Sikh who likes karaoke? Gupty Singh.

72.

A small arrowhead dating back to the Stone Age and found in a Glasgow park has been identified by archaeologists as having belonged to the tribe Wee Arra People.

73.

Where's Santa Fe? The North Pole.

74.

What did the drinker say when the bartender took his glass away? "Where did my Glasgow?".

75.

What do you call an Egyptian who drives a Glasgow taxi? Toot an come oot.

76.

What did the male Siamese twins from Glasgow call their autobiography? *Oor Wullie*.

77.

The Perishin' Poem from the pen of legendary cartoonist Bud Neill –

Winter's came, the snow has fell,
Wee Josie's nosis frozis well,
Wee Josie's frozen nosis skintit,
Winter's diabolic, intit?

78.

My dad taught me that the English upper class are sent to school to be taught to be confident, whereas in Glasgow you're born confident.
Rankin.

"Why do people say, 'Oh, you want to have your cake and eat it too?' Dead right! What good is cake if you can't eat it?" *Billy Connolly*.

A man walks into a pub in Shawlands and asks for a pint of lager with a dash of lime. "We don't do cocktails," the barman informs him.

81.

A man walks into an antiques shop and asks: "How much for the set of antlers?" £200, he is told. "That's affa deer," says the man.

82.

Bert the carpet factory foreman in Dennistoun was nicknamed Subway. He came round every five minutes.

83.

Glasgow Airport (terrorist attack), that was a mistake. Unbelievable. I think the message was learned. Don't mess with Scottish people who have a holiday booked, okay?
English comedian Michael MacIntyre.

84.

What do you call a Glasgow pigeon that goes on holiday to Aviemore? A skean dhu.

85.

A teacher asks one of his streetwise pupils:
"If you have £5 and I ask to borrow £2, how many pounds do you have left?"
"£5", the pupil answers without hesitation.

86.

Wee Isa congratulated her neighbour young Jenny on the birth of triplets. "Aye the doactor says it only happens wance in 200,000 times," says

Jenny. "Oh my Goad," gasps Wee Isa, "How did ye manage tae get ony time ti dae hoosework!"

87.

In the days when the belt was part of classroom life at his Catholic school Paul arrived home begrutten. His maw asked what was wrong and was shocked when the wee lad said he had been given six of the best for singing Away in a Manger. "Whit!", said his maw, "Ah'll away doon tae that school first thing in the morning." But Paul's dad said: "There must be mair tae it, let us hear whit ye sang Paul." The wee lad clears his throat: *Away in a manger, No crib for a bed, the little Lord Jesus He sat up and said, 'Championees, Championees! The Celts have won the Cup.'*

88.

In the child custody case following divorce proceedings Jinty McDougall declared her husband had only spoken to her three times during their marriage. She got custody of the three weans

89.

Two eggs boiling in a pan in Easterhouse.
First egg: "It's hot in here. I'll be glad to get out."
Second egg: "Don't be too anxious. When we do they'll bash our heads in."

Growing up in inner city Glasgow, it sometimes seemed to me that money had never been invented.
Jack Bruce, late bassist with rock band Cream.

I was asked by this lady if I wanted super sex.
"If its all the same to you I'll just have the soup," I replied. *Rev I M Jolly (Rikki Fulton).*

92.

Rumours of pending redundancies were rife at the shipyard. "Joabs are in Jeopardy," said Wee Harry. "Ah'm no' goin' tae work there, Ah like

Govan too much," said his mate. "Aye they're sayin' six fitters will huv tae go," said Wee Harry. Mate: "Jist as weel yir only five feet four."

Toneless singer at an old folks club in Anniesland announced: "I will now sing *On the Road to Dundee*." Fed up senior turns to pal and says: "Thank God for that, I thought he was going to attempt another one here."

A snail crawled into a bar in Maryhill and asked for a pint. The barman picked up the snail went to the door and threw it as far as he could. Nine months later the snail returned to the bar and asked: "What did you do that for?"

We had the Commonwealth Games in Glasgow. A great choice of venue – a place where people think Hepatitis B is a vitamin. *Frankie Boyle*.

The Scots are a very tough people. They have drive-by head buttings. In Glasgow, a sweatband is considered a silencer.
American comedian Emo Philips.

When I was 12, we went from Glasgow to Aberdeen on a school trip. It was called fresh air fortnight. *Billy Connolly.*

A merry band of Glesca pals were returning home following a golfing weekend on the east coast. Feeling hunger pangs, they decided to stop off at a steakhouse for a bit of scran. Asked by the waiter how he would like the his steak, one member of the band who was renowned for his voracious appetite shrugged and replied, "Ah'm no that bothered. Joost take the hoarns off and wipe its erse."

Glasgow is of course superior to Edinburgh, which is why the Edinburghers like to have a dig at Weegies when they can. Given their lack of humour some of these are not too bad. What do you call a Weegie in a suit? The accused. What do you call a Weegie in a white shellsuit? The bride. What do you say to a Weegie in a uniform? A Big Mac and fries please. How do you contact the spirit of a dear, departed Weegie? Use a Weegie board.

And finally, let's face it, Glaswegians can be a bit cruel to their own who may not be blessed with the bonniest of looks. Face like a camel eatin' sherbet. Face like a bulldog chewing a wasp. Face like a dug lickin' pish aff a nettle. Face that looks like he/she has been dookin fur apples in a chip pan. When he wis born, he wiz that ugly the doactor skelped his mammy.